Call of Duty: Warzone

Beginner's Guide

21st Century Skills **INNOVATION LIBRARY**

Josh Gregory

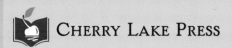
CHERRY LAKE PRESS

Published in the United States of America by Cherry Lake Publishing Group
Ann Arbor, Michigan
www.cherrylakepublishing.com

Reading Adviser: Beth Walker Gambro, MS, Ed., Reading Consultant, Yorkville, IL

Cherry Lake Press is an imprint of Cherry Lake Publishing Group.

Library of Congress Cataloging-in-Publication Data

Names: Gregory, Josh, author.
Title: Call of duty: warzone : beginner's guide / by Josh Gregory.
Description: Ann Arbor, Michigan : Cherry Lake Publishing, [2023] | Series: Unofficial guides. 21st century skills innovation library | Includes bibliographical references and index. | Audience: Grades 4-6 | Summary: "Combining the classic gameplay of the bestselling Call of Duty series with the battle royale format of games like Fortnite, Call of Duty: Warzone has become one of the biggest competitive multiplayer games in the world. In this book, readers will find out how the game was made and learn everything they need to know to succeed in online matches. Includes table of contents, author biography, sidebars, glossary, index, and informative backmatter"— Provided by publisher.
Identifiers: LCCN 2023002176 (print) | LCCN 2023002177 (ebook) | ISBN 9781668927946 (library binding) | ISBN 9781668928998 (paperback) | ISBN 9781668930465 (epub) | ISBN 9781668933428 (kindle edition) | ISBN 9781668931943 (pdf)
Subjects: LCSH: Call of duty (Game)—Juvenile literature.
Classification: LCC GV1469.35.C33 G74 2023 (print) | LCC GV1469.35.C33 (ebook) | DDC 794.8—dc23/eng/20230124
LC record available at https://lccn.loc.gov/2023002176
LC ebook record available at https://lccn.loc.gov/2023002177

Cherry Lake Publishing Group would like to acknowledge the work of the Partnership for 21st Century Learning, a Network of Battelle for Kids. Please visit http://www.battelleforkids.org/networks/p21 for more information.

Printed in the United States of America

Note from publisher: Websites change regularly, and their future contents are outside of our control. Supervise children when conducting any recommended online searches for extended learning opportunities.

Josh Gregory is the author of more than 200 books for kids. He has written about everything from animals to technology to history. A graduate of the University of Missouri–Columbia, he currently lives in Chicago, Illinois.

Contents

CHAPTER 1

Updating a Classic

In the world of video games, some series stand out as true classics. Each new entry creates a whirlwind of excitement where fans eagerly follow every bit of news they can get their hands on. For the past two decades, the Call of Duty series has been whipping game fans into a frenzy with new titles nearly every year.

For some players, Call of Duty games are the only ones they need—each one offers plenty of fun until the next is released. The games offer fast-paced multiplayer action with snappy controls that feel fun. Each one shares the same basic first-person shooter formula, but with new modes, maps, weapons, and other features to keep things fresh.

The first Call of Duty game was released way back in 2003. It was set during World War II and primarily focused on a single-player mode. The game was created by a team of **developers** at a company called Infinity Ward. At the time, Infinity Ward was a newly formed company, set up as a part of Activision, one of the world's largest video game publishers. Its developers had previously worked on games in the Medal of Honor series, another first-person shooter series set during World War II.

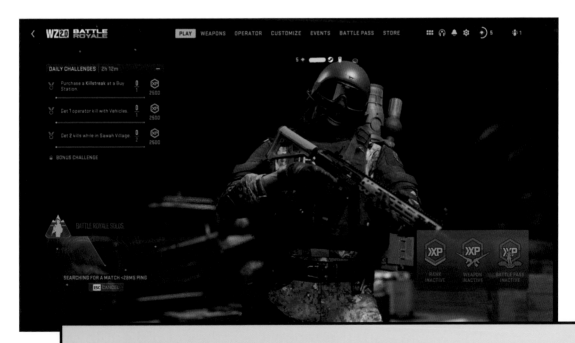

The latest Call of Duty games always feature state-of-the-art graphics.

On the Go

In March 2022, Activision announced that it was preparing a new version of *Warzone* for mobile devices. Released later that year, the game was called *Call of Duty: Warzone Mobile*. Even though some features were simplified to work on mobile phones and other devices, it offered many of the same features as the full game. The best part is that any progress players make on the mobile version syncs with the main game. This means they can truly take *Warzone* anywhere they go.

The original *Call of Duty* was very successful, selling well and earning awards and praise from critics. The next two games in the series also did very well. Both were similar to the first, with a World War II setting. But the series reached a new level of success in 2007 with the release of *Call of Duty 4: Modern Warfare*.

Unlike previous games, *Modern Warfare* was set in the near future, with advanced weapons and gear. It also introduced many new multiplayer features, such as the ability for players to gain experience points and level up. This would earn them new gear they could equip on their characters, offering new in-game abilities. Players loved this new feature; it encouraged them to keep playing and trying to reach higher and higher levels.

Modern Warfare became the highest-selling game of 2007 and earned extremely high praise from critics. Since then, the Call of Duty series has consistently been one of the biggest things in gaming. More than 400 million Call of Duty games have been sold throughout the series' history. Because each game is so huge, and they are released so frequently, Infinity Ward is no longer the only development team that works on the series. Instead, several teams rotate working on different games, sharing their work with each other as needed.

Call of Duty: Warzone lets players explore a wide variety of environments, from wilderness to huge buildings and cities.

Each Call of Duty game has featured a variety of different multiplayer game modes, ranging from simple contests to see which players can earn the most points from taking out opponents to team-based modes with complex objectives. But by the late 2010s, many gamers were getting more interested in battle royale games like *Fortnite* and *Apex Legends*. The teams behind Call of Duty decided that they should find a way to explore this new gameplay style in their own series.

The basic flow of a battle royale game is always the same: land on a map, gather loot, and outlast your opponents.

Developed by Infinity Ward alongside the team at Raven Software, *Call of Duty: Warzone* was released in 2019 as a free download. Previous Call of Duty games had all cost money to play, but *Warzone* had to compete with other free-to-play battle royale games. Even though it was up against tough competition from games like *Fortnite, Warzone* was an immediate success. Since its release, it has been downloaded by more than 125 million players around the world. About forty to fifty million people play the game each month, with more than half a million of them online at any given moment on average.

Since release, Raven Software has taken over as the primary development team behind *Warzone*. It has continually updated the game, adding new maps, improving the game's **balance**, and ironing out **bugs**. In November 2022, it released a major update called *Warzone 2.0*, which added another new map and other gameplay features alongside improved graphics for the PlayStation 5 and Xbox Series X versions of the game.

With so many exciting updates being released all the time, it's always a good time to jump in and try *Warzone* for yourself. Are you ready to drop in and start battling?

CHAPTER 2

Dropping In

If you want to try *Warzone* for yourself, all you need is a PlayStation, Xbox, or PC and a fast internet connection. It's a completely free download, though there are also **microtransactions** if you are interested in collecting the game's many **cosmetic** items.

Once you download the game and start it for the first time, you'll be sent directly to a short tutorial mode. This will teach you the basic controls of the game. If you've ever played a previous Call of Duty game, you should be pretty familiar with the way things work. Or even if you've only played other first-person shooters, a lot of the basics are the same. Use the tutorial to get used to moving around, picking up new weapons and gear, and battling against enemies.

There are several game modes available in *Warzone*, but the main one is Battle Royale. Select that from the main menu to get started with your first match. You can choose to play solo or as part of a two-, three-, or four-person team. Regardless of which one you pick, you will be facing off against a huge number of other players. *Warzone* matches can have up to 200 players, though outside of special events the number is usually 150. The object of Battle Royale is simple: be the last one standing at the end of the match.

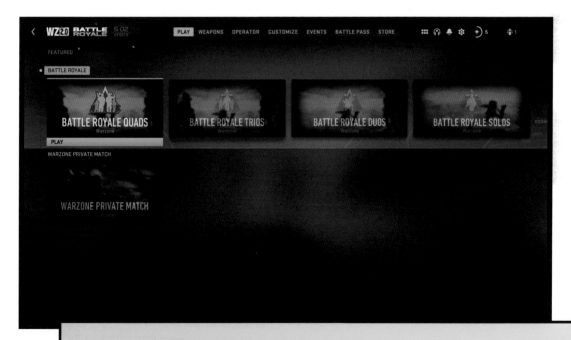

Four-person teams is the most popular form of battle royale in *Warzone*.

As you parachute down, you can see the names of different areas on the map, making it easier to figure out where you're going.

Each match will begin with everyone parachuting from an airplane down to the island below. The island is a huge place packed with all kinds of interesting locations, from towns to military bases. Where you choose to land will have a big effect on the match. However, it will take some time to learn your way around, so pick anywhere that looks interesting when you are first learning the ropes.

After jumping from the plane, you can deploy your parachute to slow down and glide toward the place you want to land. You can cut your parachute to start falling again and then redeploy your parachute as many times as you like. Use this to control how fast you fall and which direction you go. The fastest way to reach the surface is to simply free-fall and then open your parachute at the last moment.

Staying Safe

Warzone is an online game where you will regularly interact with people from all over the world. Many of them will be strangers. The best way to enjoy the game is to play with a team of friends you know from real life. That way, you can safely chat and not have to talk to anyone else. But if you end up on a team with people you don't know, you might hear them talking. Remember never to say anything about yourself online. Don't reveal where you live or go to school. And if someone says something that makes you uncomfortable, leave the game and tell an adult right away.

Once you land, your first goal is to find some gear. You'll start with a basic pistol and two armor plates. Armor plates are the blue bars above your health in the bottom left corner. You can wear up to three at a time and carry five more. Try to carry as many as you can at all times. You will need them to repair your character after taking damage in fights.

You should also seek out a weapon that is better than the starting pistol. This weapon is fine if you get into a fight right after landing, but it won't take long for your opponents to start upgrading to better gear.

Armor plates are essential for making it through battles against other players.

Your starting pistol will help you avoid getting knocked out early on, but you should find better weapons as soon as possible.

As you move around, keep an eye on your map. You have a small version of the map in the corner of your screen, but you can also pull up a full-screen version for a better look. Spend time studying it to get used to where everything is and figure out the fastest ways to get around.

Over the course of a match, as players get eliminated, a circle will close in on the map, getting smaller and smaller. You need to stay within this circle. Otherwise, your character will take damage. The better you know the map, the better your odds will be of staying in the circle.

Soon enough, you will probably end up in a battle with other players. When all of your character's health is gone, you will be knocked down. In this state, you can no longer attack. You can only move slowly. If a teammate is nearby, they can come and revive you back to fighting shape. If you have an item called a self-revive kit, you can do this yourself.

When you are downed, you will see another health bar slowly decreasing. The bar will decrease even faster if an opponent continues to attack you. If it reaches zero,

Check first aid kits on the walls of buildings for healing items.

Gulag battles are usually short and intense.

you will be eliminated from the game. But don't worry yet—you will still have a chance to get back in the action.

The first time you are eliminated, you will be sent to a location called the gulag. Here, you will face off against other recently eliminated players using basic gear. If you win, you will be dropped back onto the island for a second chance. You can also be brought back by your teammates—more on that in the next chapter.

CHAPTER 3

Going the Distance

There is a steep learning curve when it comes to getting good at *Warzone*. Unless you have a lot of experience with older Call of Duty games or you are a natural whiz at first-person shooters, you will find yourself up against very stiff competition. But don't get frustrated if you're getting knocked out seconds or minutes into every match. If you keep at it and learn some advanced strategies, you'll have a fighting chance.

First off, you should always think carefully about your gear. There are more than one hundred different weapons to find as you play, and each one has different strengths and weaknesses. Some are better in certain situations than others. For example, a sniper rifle is better than a shotgun for long-range fights. Some weapons also just do more damage than others. Weapons come in different levels of rarity, from white-colored common items to gold legendary items. Weapons of a higher rarity are almost always more powerful than more common ones. They do more damage, and they have special features like scopes that make it easier to damage opponents.

Check duffel bags, crates, and other types of loot caches to find important gear.

But when you're hunting for gear, rarity isn't the only thing to consider. You can only carry two weapons at a time. This means you should try to find two weapons that are useful in different situations. For example, if you have an assault rifle, you don't need a second one. Look for a pistol, a sniper rifle, or something else instead. This also helps you avoid running out of ammo. If you have two weapons that both use the

You will find vehicles scattered around the map, making it easier to travel long distances quickly.

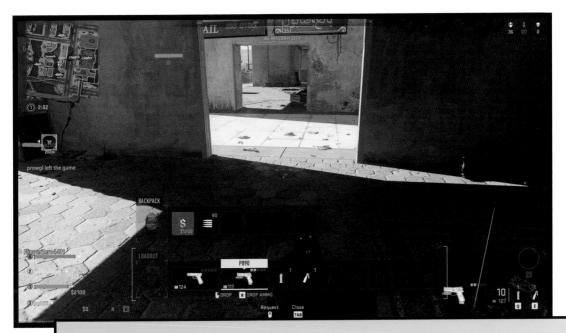

The inventory screen shows you all the items and ammo you are currently carrying.

same kind of ammo, you'll be out of luck when you run out of shots. But if your second weapon uses a different type of ammo, you can continue the fight.

You can also find items called attachments, which you can add to your weapons to change their abilities. For example, you might find a stock that makes your aim steadier, or a magazine that increases the number of shots you can take before reloading. Consider each attachment's benefits carefully when deciding which ones to use.

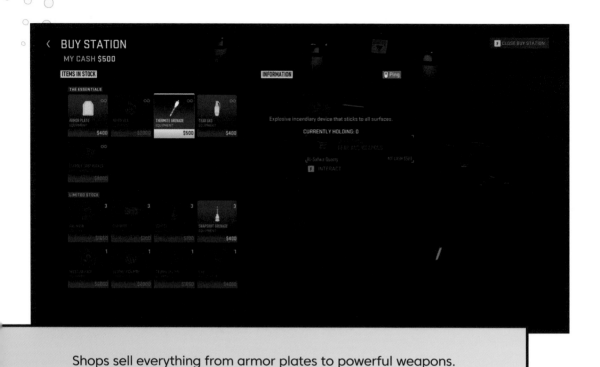

Shops sell everything from armor plates to powerful weapons.

Try to collect as much cash as possible as you move around the island. Cash can be used at special shops around the map. These look like storage lockers, but they are much more. You can spend cash to revive teammates, get powerful gear, call in airstrikes against your enemies, and more. Having a big pile of cash can completely change the course of a match.

Of course, having great gear and tons of cash is no help if you aren't skilled in the basics of combat. Cover is important in *Warzone*. If you are out in the open, other players can spot you and attack from a distance, potentially knocking you out before you have a chance to fight back. Be careful to stay in cover as much as possible. Look around before running out into the open. If you are playing with teammates, try to watch each other's backs to avoid a surprise attack.

Dodge in and out of cover quickly to make yourself harder to hit when attacking.

In general, teamwork is very important in all of *Warzone*'s team-based modes. Use the game's "ping" system to point out gear, enemies, and other useful targets to your teammates. If someone gets downed, do your best to get to them and revive them as soon as you can. You should also share weapons and gear with

The ping system shows different message options depending on what you are aiming at.

Watch What You Say

No matter what happens during a match, remember that everyone is there to have fun. Don't be mean to your teammates if they mess something up or you think they aren't playing well enough. Instead, encourage them and do what you can to help them get better at the game. Even if you are really good at the game, remember that you started out as a beginner, too. No one likes to get yelled at or be made fun of.

teammates, especially if someone is having trouble finding good equipment. You can even pool your cash together by giving it all to one member of the team. Then this member can visit a shop to get powerful bonuses that help everyone on the team.

CHAPTER 4

Fashion on the Battlefield

Like other popular online games, Warzone offers a huge range of cosmetic items for players to unlock and customize the looks of their characters. There are **skins** that change a character's overall clothing and appearance. There are also skins that change the look of different weapons. You can also unlock blueprints for new weapons to use in the game.

There are a couple of different ways to unlock new items in *Warzone*. The main way is to level up the Battle Pass. You can do this by earning experience points, or XP. You get XP for every match you play.

The better you do, the more XP you will get. You can also get XP bonuses by completing special in-game challenges, such as taking out a certain number of opponents without being knocked out yourself. Or taking out a certain number of opponents in a specific location on the map, or while using a specific weapon.

Leveling up will give you access to a wider variety of weapons and other gear.

Each time you gain enough XP to level up, you will move up a rank on the Battle Pass. Moving up ranks unlocks new items. There are two different versions of the Battle Pass: free and paid. The free version does not give you as many items as the paid version. But the good news is that if you decide to switch to the paid version when you are already partway through leveling up the Battle Pass, you will automatically receive all the items you would have unlocked so far.

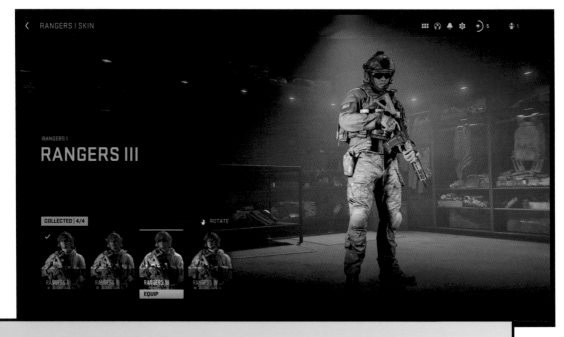

Each playable character, or operator, has a different set of available skins to choose from.

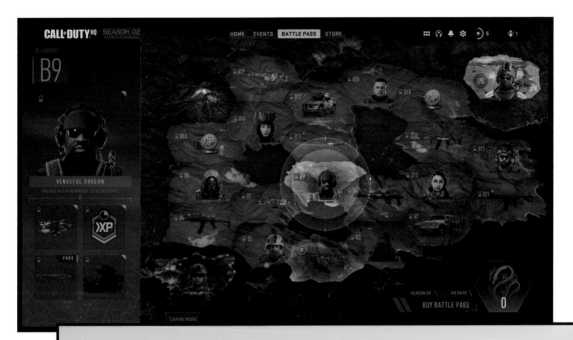

As you earn Battle Pass points, you can choose which items you want to unlock.

A new Battle Pass is added every couple of months with the introduction of a new *Warzone* season. This means that if you want all the items in a Battle Pass, you only have a limited time to unlock them.

Keep an Eye on Your Cash

Always ask an adult before spending money in *Warzone* or any other online game. Even though microtransactions might not be very expensive, they can quickly add up if you buy a lot of them. Remember that the things you buy in *Warzone* are not needed to win or have fun. Improving your skills is much more important to your success!

Aside from the Battle Pass, there is also an in-game store where you can simply purchase items directly. The items available change every day, and some are only on sale for a limited time.

Warzone's developers are always adding new cosmetics and other fun items to the game to keep longtime players interested. It's impossible to collect everything. But this never-ending variety means there is always something new to discover!

The items in the *Warzone* in-game store are sometimes based on real-life people or characters from other games and movies.

GLOSSARY

balance (BAL-uhns) the overall difficulty level and fairness of a video game's various systems and rules

bugs (BUHGS) errors in a computer program's code

cosmetic (kahz-MEH-tik) relating to how something looks

developers (dih-VEL-uh-purz) people who make video games or other computer programs

microtransactions (MYE-kroh-trans-ak-shuhns) things that can be purchased for a small amount of money within a video game or other computer program

skins (SKINS) different appearances your character can take on in a video game

FIND OUT MORE

Books

Gregory, Josh. *Careers in Esports.* Ann Arbor, MI: Cherry Lake Publishing, 2021.

Loh-Hagan, Virginia. *Video Games. In the Know: Influencers and Trends.* Ann Arbor, MI: 45th Parallel Press, 2021.

Orr, Tamra. *Video Sharing. Global Citizens: Social Media.* Ann Arbor, MI: Cherry Lake Press, 2019.

Reeves, Diane Lindsey. *Do You Like Getting Creative? Career Clues for Kids.* Ann Arbor, MI: Cherry Lake Press, 2023.

Websites

With an adult, learn more online with these suggested searches.

Call of Duty Warzone 2.0
Check out the official *Warzone* website for the latest updates on the game.

Call of Duty Wiki
This fan-created site is packed with detailed information on all of the Call of Duty games.

INDEX